LEMONS IN THE CHICKEN WIRE

LEMONS IN THE CHICKEN WIRE

ALISON WHITTAKER

To the land, and those who grow from it.

LAND-ED

land
takes dead skin from my feet
and slips
from under me
while the city
puts dead shoes on my feet
and slips
right into me

this train, the wind, ploughs on
through suburbs I barely glimpse
but there is
land and land and
I am landing

BANGERS // MASH

I was born in the boiler pot
where sausages lift their skins
turn grey, naked and barely hot
and shriek; mob eat the skin

I was born
undone
and clunky, clunky, heavy
and soft, I'd gnaw my nails half-off
and eat, I eat the skin

I was grew
rewoven
from an op shop sweater that
with clumsy, reckless love
wore fat, and with fat, thin

I was hunted
on fire
cooked, knitted and knotted
observed, but rarely wore

I was born on a warmer simmer
where potatoes would puke and foam
the starch grey, growin' thicker
I taste, I taste, I know

WILLI WILLI WILL I

I am short and curled and hot by the willi willi
in an iron-pressed check uniform
dust gusts by the mural
with brush-handle dots and acrylic lines of corroboree
I had to Google to understand

where is the diaspora of my people
when both my feet are on land?

willi willi plucked it up
and put it on the internet

EXT. INT.

My mother had a story and it would go like this:
　　　　This family is everything I hope it is to you.

My father had a story and it would go like this:
　　　　(Upstage, in garage, with car grease) Look, sure, I'd like to —

My young sister had a story and it would go like this:
　　　　Enter Relentless Violence stage left
　　　　　　　　Enter Distance and Compassion, stage (new).

My younger sister had a story and it would go like this:
　　　　Look, sis, I want to dye my hair
　　　　but I don't want to end up like you.

A FUNERAL

They dug him a metre deeper
and they put a blank slate beside his picture
where Nan waits, cleaning the rock with sugar soap
to join him in the ground.
He had a summer funeral and we all wore short skirts
I could hear him whisper 'skanks' as the ribbons wound him down. And
when a little cousin put a soft serve on his coffin
we heard, through tears
'He's lactose intolerant, you cunt!'
I kiss his picture and hope wherever he is now
that he doesn't have diarrhoea for days
when he eats a square of cheese.

INSIDER KNOWLEDGE

My pop had a joke and the joke went like this:

> There was a man and a woman in a shopping centre at Christmas, and no line to see Santa. The man said he wanted to sit on his lap, the woman did not. The joke was that they were gay.

But the joke was really that I'd been kissing Sarah from down the road, and before I told him I was the woman who didn't want to touch no Santa, Pop was dead.

My nan had a joke and the joke went like this:

> She told Pop we was kissing, so he told the joke louder at parties.

My mum had a joke and the joke went like this:

> You don't know what you are, but we do.

PREFACE : ANOTHER FUNERAL

The ground has sunk a couple of centimetres since they were
put down there
and Uncle tripped over, twisted his ankle and tried to sue
a couple deep in sleep in boxes
who can't even graze their fingers together.
Hers black from a catastrophic stroke
his gnarled from a life of slitting cows' throats
and when we come to see their grave Mum makes me pick off
my nail polish
or clasp my hands behind my back so
Great Nan don't think I'm sassing her or her passing.
You can trace the tracks round the grave with your smallest finger.
They take dirt from her grave to town and to the lives she touched
all here to mourn the strength of a woman
whose home brew landed men in hospital
whose cheese started an outbreak of listeria
who would tickle me until I pissed myself
and offer me one of her adult diapers.

CARRY THE ONE

carry the one, carry him on
tall soldier of forgotten wars
Botany Bay has a bloody floor, and still, we carry the one

I before 'e
except after sea
when the freshwater is salted for cooking
or on the plain, my peoples slain
and then 'e comes before I

skirts to the calf, recess at half past
I carry the one
and Aunt Mary's last devon roll
first blood from my uterine walls
I wait for 'e so I can come

AH

I never knew
what weight felt like
until I cut my hair
and the relief snapped my neck

I never knew
what fate felt like
until of all the possibilities
it was the tonne of feathers that hit me

I never knew
what late looked like
until the first time in Koori time
Mum came home early
to crushed shrubs beneath my window

CINNAMON EGGS

mighty hungry and mighty matte, the bike is crusted
cinnamon, rusted
wedged by a hollow tree and grass pushed flat

the chooks are quiet
the day is a sputtering oven
the sun rising and spinning, fan-forced and
I, the lemon, split at the segments
am curling and fragranced and short-shortsed

and helmeted. And seizing the bike and
coaxing it down
a narrow pressed track

this shuddering bike knows my body like it built it
on it I'd spilled myself out twenty-eight times
to the new moon
separately, twenty-eight times
this bike had cut bitumen right into my blood
it slammed tar into my teeth 'til I was a gourmand
who knew
the palatable distinctions of north-west floors
and two grams in my knees for the joint to gnaw

the bike is hungry for that dirt, but I'm hungrier for it still
my grating knees give chase

a trail of bike scabs scintillates
pickles and burns mid-air
as the fan-forced day spins on

at a startle bump
my foot slips free on fresh bike skin

I twist and collapse, metres from the camp
a whimpered, veiny shriek
paling fist, and bike seat damp

the milky wafer I'd tried to shove tampons behind —
that taut aperture I'd tried to coax myself behind
(at the thought of she) (without success)
has split
the twenty-ninth bleeding moot/the first to a half-moon

bare feet on the cinnamon scab trail
my sister gawks with horror at my bloody shorts
and the bird nest I crushed

eyes darting for explanation
between the eggs
whitening in the heat of the grass-road hem
and me
flushed, torn and limping 'sif I laid 'em

TASTE A // VERSE

My mother lets me lap tea at seven; she brews it with two teabags
one Lipton, one Dilmah
for ten minutes and lets me at it
it is bitter and floury, like licking a damper kneading board
I tell her I hate tea and she says
            thank god, another jar saved from smashing.

My father feeds me strawberries at eight
I think he feeds me the green ones, cheekily
sour and acerbic
            the little brat be touching adult food no more.

At nineteen someone feeds me strawberries
real ones, plump with redness and weeping and drunk
            my god, they're still disgusting.

At twelve, my mother makes me tea with damper and jam
and lashings of milk;
            I relish it and I know that something else bitter is coming.

WHATCHA

Whatcha bleedin' in the bath for, girl?
Don't kid me, I can see it
See, there, a clot near the drain 'ole
And your cunt pashed the rim while you were shavin'

Look at it, I can see the whole thing
All splayed out like a wound
Hey, whatcha wipin' it with a towel for?
You know them towels are yellow, girl?

And what's your father gonna think when he sees 'em?
That you cut yourself shavin' your moot?
What's your father gonna think if he thinks you shavin' it?
That youse some skank around town?

I can see a tampon wrapper on the ground, girl
And you better grab it quick smart
Put it in the bathroom bin, girl
And spray the air when you is done

What happens when your friends smells your cunt rags, girl?
You'll be scarrin' 'em for life
Whatcha doin' not showerin' when you's bleedin', girl?
And not usin' a separate bar of soap?

GROWING SOON

I imagined my mother
like all daughters
imagine their sister
with curly hair like mine
and growing up with me

I imagined my father
like all sons
imagine a collared shirt
with a red-rust neck rim
keen and perspiring

my mother imagined me
like all children
imagine a bad influence
with good grades, but
thick neck, tattooed

my father imagined me
like all sunsets
dyed red and yellow
and distant
and going soon

THE STICKING PLACE

Last nights make a gluey bubble
in thin crepe expansive time
tonight I watch that lingering bubble
cloud the moon, and mine the light.

Here time is halted, as if the earth
stopped turning to gaze at a lover
you turn your gaze to country
mournfully, feet curled into the earth
aware that dawn waits to prise you.

But time, it stands back-to-back with you
and it leans, and sometimes you
gain momentum with its weight, other times
it's a limp carcass whose shoulders dislocate.

This night, time is still
a warm, soundless bubble
shrouds dread of the morning.

The last night on country
you bury yourself in the earth under time's weight
to hold this touch
you gasp it, gasp it, eat it.

FLORA

the following is a list of native flowers:
wattle
kangaroo paw
waratah
pink heath (common)

the following is a list of native flowers:
sarah (first kiss)
kayla (first love)
marticia (no love)
tayla (common)

the following is a list of native flowers:
entreaty
warmth
achey heels
hayfever (common)

the following is a list of introduced fauna:
rabbits
foxes
christmas lights on fire in the dirt
hayfever (uncommon)

FAUNA

Bulbs pop in the dirt. Your skin is seasoned
with glass and
tungsten shards

unharmed but
there is a sense
that life is slowing
like a wounded animal by roadside
draining of fear

LEMONS : METAPHOR

Lemons: metaphor
juicy, weeping, squirting, tart
flanked neighbour's orchard

THE FIRST COOLEST THING

if she's wearing thick lip gloss
you'll feel it on your face
when you're on the bus for hours
back to your nan's place

if she's wearing glasses
there'll be a cut right on your cheek
where the blackfulla line creases
her mug pushed right to yours
it'll be there for a week

if she's wearing your skin
you'll feel it maybe somewhere
like when an elevator sinks
suddenly
you are electric

if she's wearing fists
you'll feel it on your face
when you're on the dole
and-shamed-and
back to your nan's place

THE SECOND COOLEST THING

no one tells you that it's slight

flies grazing over finger hairs
adrenal-thin, moist breath ensnares
nerves raw with life and slick with sweat
a cigarette-framed silhouette
and jittered skips of fetid hearts
as fog, two breaths, and then departs

two moths, we welded by the teeth
to bumble in the wealthy east
a modest crime for the meagre feast

SMELLS LIKE WHISTLING

I know him well, the synasthete
with globules of wondrous light for feet
with hair tossed brown ashiver, cry'n
moving like the graphed cosine, an'

I know him well, the mottled toe
the locus, radius, lieu and fro'
cocoons himself in things that reek
of the colour blue, and slime of leek

I know him well, the bursting ruck
the elbow spit, the weeping luck
limes brown as he cries
they pucker, pips burst from his eyes

he knows me, I'm a milky girl
knows nebulae, my drunken hurl
the skateboard ramp, my naked back
he tastes, he tastes, that I am black

MARDI GRASS

never lived Brokeback
I understand though
secretive longing
the pinky to palm
nipples to cheap bra
Mardi Gras, compared
is cruelly full

grass blade to the mouth
a cliché but I
miss the hot enclaves
of mob queers on the fringe
greying sensual fields
unpinnable space
devon-stuffed closets

chasing young peewees
texting with scab knees
prouder than I'll ever
be, again
'twixt the Mardi Grass

SCRAG LIT

The first queer book I'd scrounged from the library
had a cluster of sticks on the cover, anyway, I read a story in it
 that said
to feel love is to relish the emptiness of a body
the seconds when a lover pulls away from you
at fourteen, I thought that, surely!
my perpetual emptiness
and sparseness of my yellowing world meant
that I had known the limit of my loving.

By fifteen, I was frightened that all I could love was this
 stretching lack
that all like me were damned to have
a desperate, vacant love, not like desire, but like
starving, with a mouth burnt from soup
waiting, for it to cool.

-ING; -LY

I sucked her fingers one by one
where I lingered, rings of lipstick stayed
on one knuckle, then another
hot and red and suddenly
sticky
like a surprise cut
red marks like keen slices
as if she moved them, presently
they would split at the joint
like a doll whose ball sockets rotted
dislodge into my throat
gut
and choke me
instantly

WATTLE IN THE DYKES

pest wattle juts from the dyke
waxy pollen firework; intervention on the flood plain
draining the mould from home

the death flower perched within the garage dykes
to curse the whole damned house

I put it there
and there it burns

cocky and daring, and caught by flame
bright, then ash in the gutter
house damned all the same

FROM SIRENS, THE STORM SETTLES

sound drips in blisters
now droops with silence — let it
magpie groans — let it

NACL

here, I lash salt to the water to clean the weeping splits
left by the stinging bush, and the burr citadel

all the flavour I can grasp in this freshwater town is salted radishes
and river yellowbelly
and cut up feet

elsewhere, she
licks this salt right off the border between my palm and hand
where the latter pores get coarse and sprout hairs
a lemon
tequila
I'm faint

and to the harbour we fall in, salt
and in other things, salt

she mines the salt water and as we dry —
her hair and I are stiff with it

SILVER PILLOW

I am close to bursting when you lie on my chest

we're dull, and with dullness matted
like hair coasters, dadaist fur objects
drinking and infected from the hairy cup

blasé, naff, artisanal, bored dykes watching sitcoms
cold, mad in the shadows and on your mother's couch
we lie but never rest

you tell me you will grow a moustache
I read a shampoo bottle and hack up a tea leaf

a tired warmth blooms
and from the seams, lavendered domestic hope

[H]EARTH

I know it's cold at home
when her nipples peak
like cliff-bounded hills that guard the river

I hold a warmer groan
when brown breads creak
and then split. We butter the slivers

I know it's cold at home
when my hands sheath
I am frightened of her eyes and her brown
hair

I know it's warm at home
when the forecast is bleak
and the hearth burns the whole street down
there

RE- ; IN-

nipples in a linen shirt
tight with blood, gaze downward
trace a jawline with a thigh
clumsy and indelicate

sitting in an open fridge
forehead in the crisper
she shatters frozen lettuce with her hand and wipes it on the tile
the grout sands her fingernails
the whole earth her emery board
perpendicular to her will
eagerly shifting with the gravity of a
woman stoned, her gaze downward and shoulders like cliffs
she talks about collarbones
and how they grow rings
like trees
or a yule log
or a married couple

I, by stove top
refrying frozen chips
while the microwave drones on
like a drawn out heartbeat
an elongated punctual clap
vibrating through my knee
now until the end of time

ESSAY, DISSOLVED

'gainst the glass, my voice lowers, and softens, the vowels elongate, slither into my nasal passages.

Sentence structure flakes.

> I shed the metalanguage somewhere near Kuring-Gai, a collection of gender theories which serve to facilitate the multiplicity of queerness.
>
> The 'g' drops off the suffix 'ing'. The arch of my sentences morphs. Prepositions disappear.

Slang?

Ham wallets, boner-dykes and breeders were left by the edge of the platform at the smoke break, where a butch with crude charm slouches and smirks an all-pervasive smirk of queer disclosure, demystified, desacralised, and fills my clothes with second-hand queer and smoke.

I'm not passing. Is it how I'm walking, talking, dressing? Is it the way I'm being?

HEAVY TONGUE

Ngaya yarrbun maa
dhalay ngay gababala
wiyaybaa yinarr

Ngaya,

am clumsy
better my tongue
foreigner Aboriginal woman

I

THE DOUBLE MIRROR

Suleri said the colonised
(in humid rooms, plucking affray socks from low slow-cutting
fans)
were seduced by scratched-out, published minds
(tongue-dried, red-pored and dust-swallowed, I gripped my
glands)
which turned they to themselves. The tender hope of literature
(fucked neck, on the four two two, half-watching our
reflections in the window)
throwing paint into place, to glue the black on the pre-colonial picture
(myself watching him watching me, he stifles a grin and takes a
photo)
she said we now had no eyes or tongue. In the squinting light, our
calcified history
(I wonder where it goes, who he shows
The Bus Bitch/Lardo/Coon.jpg)
demarcated, cannot rescue us from the gaze of another
(I put on lipstick for this shit?)

O, EUREKA!

A scalp-scab burnt and straw-haired woman
spoke to me a revolution
that roared within my belly, only once it were ate
after years of pushin' it round the plate
and when I realised what she knew
and what I missed — O, Eureka!

Nan sliced her finger on a crossword
and wrote with that a dissertation, then she
browning, spoke to me
her contested trinity
the messianic, and the self, and the
blades of grass that pierce the pulp
of weedy toes, that the world should meet you
and wound you as you wound it
made Descartes wrong about that split
O, Eureka!

And O,
the first time I said
a long white theory word
she yarned stiff to impress me
like, with that word
came authority, and with it, fear
that she had been misunderstood
her praxis clumsy or unheard
O, the weaker!

And then, at every drawn goodbye
like a choir, leaning each to the other to hold a clap
my nan clasps my hands and whispers to me
decolonising epistemology, and
critical autonomy, and
affective phenomenology.

And what she says is:
remember yourself, and call me once a week
on which I ruminate
O, Eureka!

SHARP TONGUE

CORNER BOOKS
BROWN & MAINE STREET

TAX INVOICE:

GAMILARAAY TO
ENGLISH DICTIONARY
$39.00

GAMILARAAY LEARNING
GUIDE $64.00

TOTAL $104.00
(INCL GST)

YOU WERE SERVED BY
AMY 26/03/2015 13:24

My tongue will catch on this
page && drag slow

&& I will make a seam of
myself

&& in this seam, I'll stuff
seeds // eggs // spores

Sewn up w/ stick && grass
&& loose thread spools

Speaking, the noisy wound will
burst

&& with that, my willi
willi-plucked tongue be born

Either that or bloody && salty
&& a monument to the last

ATRIPLEX CINEREA

grey saltbush, with pods that open like envelope eyes
there are photosynthesising oysters inside it
there are fermenting secrets inside you

you are the namesake of succulence
Truganinni
warmth in the time of cruelty
cruelty in the time of cruelty

how does the atriplex cinerea burn?
ripe with water, and with smoke
and does the atriplex cinerea rebirth?
or are its seeds and secrets scattered
to set alight other worlds?

separated by the D'Entrecasteaux often and British Channels once
your stern diplomacy saved a few
it is complex
your daughters are hardened by it
the same, the same
again, again

THE BODY COUNTRY

Tell me about the body colony, then call my thick nose pretty.

Trace the blackfulla lines under my eyes, slip through them to
the centre of my cheeks, and speak how our ancestors made homes
here, tracing the currents as they flowed north.

Walk with me, flat-footed me and flat foot and me, down the
banks of the creek tell me my flat feet will lead us somewhere,
indelicate somewhere I, indelicate, somewhere.

Say to me that you won't forget all the dusky mismatched
pigment, fat flesh, symbols on my mongrel body that survived
the frontier wars.

That mark me as Gomeroi, but in the gritty city city city
make me 'ugly waijine girl'.

Talk to me about decolonising the body then call my thick nose pretty.

COME BACK BLACK

her cheap thongs bore the grit
I hungered to have under my nails
could I cup the rubble in my hands? Drink from it,
build a new town?
into the grout
into the cracks
of cafe tiles
falls the sachet sample of the old world
dead dirt from the north-west and my mother wants me home
for Christmas

all I think of are the thongs
they swung from opaque and milky feet
hard from spilling feet and hot tar

I've piccolo latte in one hand, gammon sandwich in the other
her pink eyes flit to me, then her mother

and then she says t'me
come back

I heard the limp thongs thump and smack
her nail-less toe beds heave and slack
to this silent rhythm, foot out and back
come back black, come back black

JIM'S CARPET CLEANING

Our dirt is old now
it sticks to young toes then to
floors and memories

BIG SMOKE

by his small square house near the Namoi
my mighty pop is filled and unfilling
flushed with smoke and now
awaiting death with oxygen tank

as he deflates
he is large with self

then the Namoi inhales, capillary-less
with cascading lungs
that old myth;
without trolleys and abandoned lounges
this river's banks would wilt
has some weight on me now

without the debris
it and we
are small with self

from the small square house a torrent springs
howling mob unfill from softening man
dense, osmotic, we mob detritus
spill to the Namoi, and it floods with us

THE TENDER SHEDS

I bid:

a ribbed white singlet
a half-crafted wooden box
two cheap ceramic cherubs whose
acrylic lips drip down their chins.

And maybe:

the first bud from a flowering fern
a hidden jar of my baby teeth
every knot pulled from my hair
that brittle moment when a secret is unfurled
and breath pauses in reply.

For:

an iron wall through which rain might sieve
and rust that spreads like fire
and that the tender sheds might be just that
a crevasse within which these stoic men
could explosively rejoice, or cry.

DOGS

the dog Nan's neighbour poisoned, he was yappin' at the chooks
plodding round the camp, round the house, an' by the brook
a brown drooping observer, shadow-struck, *please don't look*

a dog loved me; he had an ugly underbite like mine
he sat outside and heard the yells, the triumphs and the like
I wished I loved him more, loved him truer, loved in time

the dog Nan's neighbour didn't kill, he don't bite me anymore
his eyes are dead opaque, won't be finding me at all
we sit beneath the house, willi willi sweep from north

he is old and I am olding and he is blind and I am finding
Nan calls for Rover, and the feasting dogs are roving

TIDDA // JIDGJA

My tidda
in the RTA
in with a riotous
and vocal complaint
you'll get your new plates soon.

My tidda
in the car fast and passing
working two jobs to make rent
I have seen you
the air you breathe will keep.

My tidda
in the bargain rack
stretching your budget
to feed a whole mob
the hungry kids are grateful.

My tidda
in the classroom
learning about Cook
but not Pemulwuy
your nan remembers, and so will you.

My tidda
in the scrubland
with great-grandchildren like a cloud 'round you
great is your power
you have suckled a mob to life.

My tidda
in the clinic
stretching the budget
to stay alive
my heart beats with yours, and strong.

My tidda
in the ground
with a custom headstone
and cheap fake flowers
they fade, but not you, no.

EPILOGUE : A FUNERAL

There is no dirt on the continent
sufficient to hold her body down
always rising toward the ceiling
in celestial white hospital sheets for fifteen years, floating in an ocean
of her own pain.

The grass won't grow over the road base they used instead
and even the white stencilled cross makes you wither with her scowl
her forget-me-not fake lillies
'Don't you fuckin' forget me or forget to feed my dog!'

(How could we forget when the funeral's recorded
and lives evermore on Facebook?)

Nevertheless her crevassed hands
gently lingered with us
in the broiling heat, there's comfort in
her careful, silent iciness.

When her husband collapsed with grief and the ambulance came
and a cousin broke her water
and two days later, when the lemon sun began to melt her grave's tar
I was sent a photo of a great-grandchild
swaddled in an orange blanket, black
and his scalp white like the crescent moon.

SIX FEET THUNDER

Three graves by a rising moon
white hot in the sinking day
the freckled moon will weep tonight
for now, he cracks a straining, crescent smile
Nan says it means he'll pour out rain.

Under solar lights
the sentinel bodies lay
while fake roses yearn for heaven
and the bleaching wash of a lemon sun.

Tempest at the Wake
Iced Pepsi Max. In
three half-glasses, floored. Woman
pregnant, howls a name

DO YA?

Do you think that tenderness lies at the end of this?
When ankle pins like Christ wounds tether
you, with motion, to the road? Perhaps wherever

that motion yanks you, there will be tenderness
if only where your wounds become a fat, soft mess.
What awaits us when this ends — pleasure?

Do you think: the marrow moves, light
like the arrow moves? If there might
be effervescent somethingness
pocketed outside of this?

Do you think the steady queue
stretching 'til their clothes soak through
loving, aching, ever knew
that something was amiss?

Do you think that tenderness lies at the end of this?
Some bleak gate guarded by whoever
waiting, parka'd in th' cold forever?

COUNTRYLINK X-PLORER : A HIGH SCHOOL ESSAY

This is not my tongue. The people here speak a different tongue and treat with serene indifference what I do with mine.

But I travel, ritualistically, seasonally, culturally, on a locus imprecisely traced by carriages like vertebrae, when I am baramaay, and retire to home.

The train shifts between two places and two selves. There was a time when I would say that this train would stretch like a sugar snake and split
one self would stretch back
the other would be eaten.

Culture (n), ritualistic
harvests collective experience
the exclusivity of spirals, dots and borders.
        Rainbows.

Some time ago, I caught this train and on it stretched out my self.
        Eclipsin'
        Queer, encryptin'
        Black.

I said things like: queerness, Aboriginality
would rather turn each other inside out
to make their meaning make me
            than let me turn inside of them
            for any measly, thin security.

And though I cannot pinpoint it
through this quick, imprecise shift
            ing
like a flipbook, merged two tired selves
'til each fed the other.
Now, when I'm on this train
I travel to culture (v) where I land like spores caught on the wind.

THREE-TIER

at first
you must embalm yourself
pull the blue network from your wrist and find the one that goes
  right back
follow that vein to the you-know-when, where it finds a black
woman in the scrub; where horror ringbarked the roots
or take that vein and point to the tier with that first sepia picture
where white film couldn't translate black smiles
(the stiffer, the better)

that picture must stiff smile back and
say you're black and
buy you your first drink; let's!
that second tier of trinkets
novelty tit mugs from Coffs Harbour, and signed champagne
  flutes
(used once with goon)
(unsubtle hints they know you)

now, this third thing about being black
is that the third tier should be poignantly vacant
you should fall on it
and read your dusty imprint
and know the weight of self
without crushing the shelf

CHICKEN WIRE LEMONS

the border is a lemon pip
and it shivers to the touch
opaque with strain
'tween fingers, lain
heaves citrus and bursts up

we was livin' to the border
and the pips they was my finger
peaked and glanced
barbed, wired and fenced
to the tip, it bleeds and lingers

and then livin' to the border
what strength, what tepid joy
to think of skin
bound to black flesh
and, thick within
the wide-eyed fresh
and to begin
to snip the mesh
of chicken wire. Joy!

oh, livin' to the border
and threading one arm through
to pluck a blacker lemon
kissing girls and eating devon
from the dirt, my bread to leaven
every push, the hole is grew

ABOUT THE AUTHOR

Alison Whittaker is a Gomeroi multitasker from the floodplains of Gunnedah. She is a Fulbright scholar, and a poet and essayist whose work has been published in *The Sydney Review of Books*, *Seizure*, *Overland*, *Westerly*, *BuzzFeed*, *Griffith Review*, *The Lifted Brow* and *Meanjin*. In 2017 she was awarded the Overland Judith Wright Poetry Prize. In 2018, Alison published *blak work*.

First published 2016, reprinted 2017, 2018
New edition 2019, reprinted 2020, 2021
Magabala Books Aboriginal Corporation, Broome, Western Australia
Website: www.magabala.com Email: sales@magabala.com

Magabala Books receives financial assistance from the Commonwealth Government through the Australia Council, its arts advisory body. The State of Western Australia has made an investment in this project through the Department of Local Government, Sport and Cultural Industries. Magabala Books would like to acknowledge the support of the Shire of Broome, Western Australia.

This manuscript won the State Library of Queensland's 2015 black&write! Indigenous Writing Fellowship, a partnership between the black&write! Indigenous Writing and Editing Project and Magabala Books.

Cover – Jo Hunt
Typeset – Post Pre-Press
Printed and bound in Australia by Griffin Press

National Library of Australia Cataloguing-in-Publication entry
Whittaker, Alison, author.
Lemons in the Chicken Wire/Alison Whittaker.
978-1-925936-89-6